Science and Technology for Children BOOKS™

Land and Water

National Science Resources Center

THE NATIONAL ACADEMIES Smithsonian Institution

National Science Resources Center

The establishment of the National Science Resources Center (NSRC) by two of the nation's most prestigious institutions, the Smithsonian Institution and the National Academies, provides the United States with a unique resource for catalyzing change in science education. The NSRC is an organization of the Smithsonian Institution and the National Academies; its mission is to improve the learning and teaching of science in the nation's school districts. The NSRC disseminates information about exemplary teaching resources, develops curriculum materials, and conducts outreach programs of leadership development, technical assistance, and professional development to help school districts implement research-based science education programs for all K–12 students.

Smithsonian Institution

One of the NSRC's parent organizations is the Smithsonian Institution. The Smithsonian Institution was created by an act of Congress in 1846 "for the increase and diffusion of knowledge...." This independent federal establishment is the world's largest museum complex and is responsible for public and scholarly activities, exhibitions, and research projects nationwide and overseas. Among the objectives of the Smithsonian is the application of its unique resources to enhance elementary and secondary education.

The National Academies

The National Academies are also a parent organization of the NSRC. The National Academies are nonprofit organizations that provide independent advice to the nation on matters of science, technology, and medicine. The National Academies consist of four organizations: the National Academy of Sciences, the National Academy of Engineering, the Institute of Medicine, and the National Research Council. The National Academy of Sciences was created in 1863 by a congressional charter. Under this charter, the National Research Council was established in 1916, the National Academy of Engineering in 1964, and the Institute of Medicine in 1970.

This book is one of a series that has been designed to be an integral component of the Science and Technology for Children® curriculum, an innovative, hands-on science program for children in grades kindergarten through six. This program would not have been possible without the generous support of federal agencies, private foundations, and corporations. Supporters include the National Science Foundation, the Smithsonian Institution, the U.S. Department of Defense, the U.S. Department of Education, the John D. and Catherine T. MacArthur Foundation, the Dow Chemical Company Foundation, the Amoco Foundation, Inc., DuPont, the Hewlett-Packard Company, the Smithsonian Institution Educational Outreach Fund, and the Smithsonian Women's Committee.

Acknowledgments

Land and Water is part of a series of books for students in kindergarten through sixth grade, and it is an integral part of the Science and Technology for Children® (STC®) curriculum program. The purpose of these books is to enhance and extend STC's inquiry-based investigations through reading. Research has shown that students improve their reading skills when challenged with interesting and engaging reading materials. In the process, key science concepts that students have been learning can be reinforced. The Teacher's Guide that accompanies the STC program gives some information on how to integrate this book with the program's inquiry-centered investigations. Those students interested in reading these books on their own will find them easy to read as stand-alone texts. All students will especially enjoy reading about highlights of the Smithsonian Institution's varied and unique museums.

The book has undergone rigorous review by experts in the field to ensure that all the information is current and accurate. A nationally recognized reading specialist has worked with us to create stories that are at a reading level that is appropriate for students in fourth and fifth grades. We have also varied the reading level throughout the book so that all students—no matter what their reading proficiency—can find stories that are both interesting and challenging.

The NSRC greatly appreciates the efforts of all the individuals listed below. Each contributed his or her expertise to ensure that the book is of the highest quality.

Science and Technology for Children Books: *Land and Water*

National Science Resources Center Staff and Consultants

Sally Goetz Shuler
Executive Director

Marilyn Fenichel
Managing Editor (consultant)

Linda Harteker
Senior Editor (consultant)

Heather Dittbrenner
Copy Editor (consultant)

Gail Peck
Designer (consultant)

Heidi M. Kupke
Graphic Designer

Max-Karl Winkler
Illustrator

John Norton
Assistant Illustrator (consultant)

Christine Hauser
Photo Editor

Susan Tannahill
Webmaster and Database Specialist

Kimberly Wayman
Procurement and Financial Assistant

Research and Development Staff and Advisors

David Marsland
Co-Director, Professional Development Center
NSRC

Henry Milne
Co-Director, Professional Development Center
NSRC

Sonya Berger
Park Ranger
National Park Service
Washington, DC

Don Garner
Weeks Drilling and Pump Company
Sonoma, CA

Andrew K. Johnston
Geographer
Center for Earth and Planetary Studies
National Air and Space Museum
Smithsonian Institution
Washington, DC

Ted A. Maxwell
Associate Director for Collections and Research
National Air and Space Museum
Smithsonian Institution
Washington, DC

Lynne Murdock
Natural Resource Interpretive Specialist
National Park Service
Washington, DC

Timothy R. Rose
Museum Specialist
Department of Mineral Sciences
National Museum of Natural History
Smithsonian Institution
Washington, DC

Bob Ryan
Chief Meteorologist
NBC4
Washington, DC

Thomas E. Simkin
Curator
Department of Mineral Sciences
National Museum of Natural History
Smithsonian Institution
Washington, DC

Karen Prestegaard
Associate Professor
Department of Geology
University of Maryland
College Park, MD

James Zimbelman
Geologist
Center for Earth and Planetary Studies
National Air and Space Museum
Smithsonian Institution
Washington, DC

Annemarie Sullivan Palincsar
Jean and Charles Walgreen Professor of Reading and Literacy
School of Education
University of Michigan
Ann Arbor, MI

Ian MacGregor
President
Science Education Associates
Berkeley, CA

Bruce Molnia
Geologist
U.S. Geological Survey
Reston, VA

Judith White
Curriculum Developer
STC Discovery Decks
Berkeley, CA

Carolina Biological Supply Company Staff

Dianne Gerlach
Director of Product Development

David Heller
Department Head, Product Development

Robert Mize
Department Head, Publications

Jennifer Manske
Publications Manager

Gary Metheny
Editor

Cindy Morgan
Senior Curriculum Product Manager

Science and Technology for Children BOOKS™

Land and Water

CONTENTS

p. 13

p. 23

p. 34

p. 42

ABOVE—PHOTO CREDITS: (FROM TOP) SMITHSONIAN INSTITUTION ARCHIVES, RECORD UNIT 7281, WILLIAM F. FOSHAG COLLECTION, NEG. #98-3307; PHOTO BY GEOFFREY DE VERTEUIL, 1996; KAREN PRESTEGAARD, UNIVERSITY OF MARYLAND, COLLEGE PARK; UNITED STATES GEOLOGICAL SURVEY PHOTO ARCHIVE

COVER—PHOTO CREDITS: (FROM TOP LEFT, CLOCKWISE) TERRY J. ADAMS, NATIONAL PARK SERVICE; GRAND CANYON NATIONAL PARK, NATIONAL PARK SERVICE; RICHARD FISKE, NATIONAL MUSEUM OF NATURAL HISTORY, SMITHSONIAN INSTITUTION

Introduction

The land and the water are always changing. Water flows over the land, carving valleys and wearing down the landscape. Forces inside Earth move continents, build mountains, and cause volcanic eruptions and earthquakes. If no rain falls, our water supplies dry up, and the land becomes cracked and parched.

THE STORIES IN PART 1 look closely at the land. Millions of years ago, Earth looked very different from the way it looks today. By studying soil and rocks very carefully, scientists called geologists were able to figure out how Earth changed, and why. Today, as scientists study natural disasters such as earthquakes and volcanoes, they are able to better understand how movement inside Earth continues to change our planet.

THE STORIES IN PART 2 focus on water. Not only do these stories explain characteristics of water, they also describe the tools scientists have to study it. For example, scientists called hydrologists use surveying equipment to determine the size and the shape of a stream. Engineers use rigs to drill for water underground.

Water, however, is more than just a substance to be studied. It is closely linked to people and how they live. The two stories at the end of this section explore people's dependence on water. *Chinese River Painting* shows how water moved people to create intricate paintings and write beautiful poetry. *The Dust Bowl* describes what happened to the land during a terrible drought and what people had to do to bring the land back before rain fell once again.

PART 3 ILLUSTRATES how closely linked the land and water are. The connection between the two influences weather. In the 19th century, a scientist named Joseph Henry first explored how weather could be forecast and how people could receive those forecasts in the most efficient way. Technology of the 21st century has greatly improved both our ability to predict the weather and ways to communicate those forecasts.

The land and the water are far more than just areas of study for scientists. They also are a source of inspiration. For example, explorers in the 1800s ventured into wild territory to run the treacherous rapids of the rivers flowing through the Grand Canyon. Today, some people consider caves the last frontier, and they go underground to learn about how they formed. Painters and poets look to rivers and land formations as a starting point for their creative work.

As you read these stories, look around where you live. Can you see mountains? Is there enough water? Do you see signs of how the land has changed over time?

 If you see this icon in the upper right-hand corner, it's a story about scientists and the work they do.

PART 1

How Earth Changes

COURTESY OF THE EARTHQUAKE ENGINEERING RESEARCH INSTITUTE

You will read the following stories in Part 1:

- **Our Moving Planet**
- **Something's Shaking**
- **Volcano in a Cornfield**
- **Rocks in Our World**

Each story explores what causes the land to change. The section opens with a

What is the relationship between Pangaea and a building toppled by an earthquake? If you don't know the answer now, you will after you finish reading the four stories in Part 1.

story explaining how scientists figured out that Earth's continents are always slowly moving across the planet's surface. These moving plates lead to two kinds of natural disasters—earthquakes and volcanoes.

The last story illustrates how different types of rocks may be used in the construction of buildings. The rocks have different properties and look quite different. The national monuments in Washington, D.C., are built with three kinds of rocks—igneous, sedimentary, and metamorphic. Find out how the properties of rocks determine how they are used.

Our Moving Planet

Earth today

This is a map showing what the world's continents look like today. Alfred Wegener used a map like this one as a starting point for his hypothesis.

Often important scientific discoveries are made because one individual is curious. Alfred Wegener was one such individual. He was a German scientist who lived in the early part of the 20th century. He looked closely at a world map and noticed that the coasts of Africa and South America looked as though they could have once fit together, much like the pieces of a jigsaw puzzle.

Alfred Wegener was a German meteorologist, a scientist who studies the weather. In 1912, he developed his hypothesis about why the continents change over time.

Take a look at this map of the world. Trace the continents of Africa and South America. Do you see what Wegener noticed?

Wegener's Hypothesis

After studying a map, Wegener developed a hypothesis to explain what happened to the continents. A hypothesis is a possible explanation for the way things are. Wegener suggested that all the continents were once joined together in a single landmass, or supercontinent. Wegener called this giant continent Pangaea.

Wegener thought that Pangaea formed about 300 million years ago. ▸

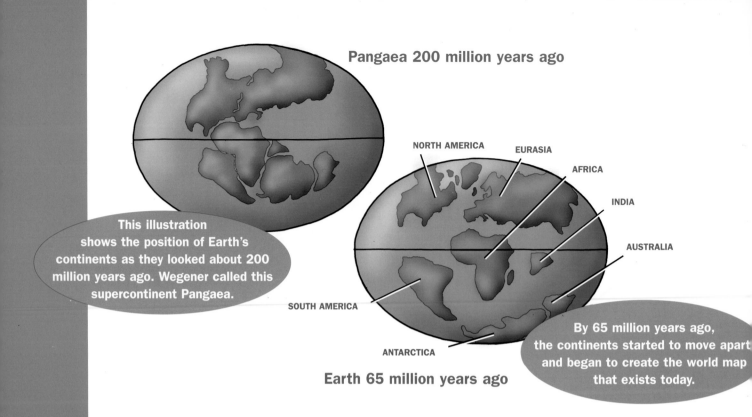

Pangaea 200 million years ago

This illustration shows the position of Earth's continents as they looked about 200 million years ago. Wegener called this supercontinent Pangaea.

NORTH AMERICA
EURASIA
AFRICA
INDIA
AUSTRALIA
SOUTH AMERICA
ANTARCTICA

Earth 65 million years ago

By 65 million years ago, the continents started to move apart and began to create the world map that exists today.

Over time, the pieces of Pangaea drifted apart. South America and Africa moved away from each other. North America separated from Europe and moved apart. This process continued until the continents looked the way they do today. Wegener's hypothesis that the continents slowly moved became known as continental drift.

How did Wegener support his theory? First, he looked at the shores of the continents. He was one of the first to notice that they matched. He also noticed that mountains that were about the same age and made of similar rocks were now found on different continents. Finally, Wegener saw evidence in fossils found around the world. For example, he was aware that fossils of two similar large reptiles were found on continents now separated by oceans. Because neither reptile could have swum across the ocean, the most logical explanation is that these continents were once a single landmass.

Wegener took his idea one step farther. He tried to explain that other changes came about as a result of continental drift. He thought that as drifting continents collided, their edges crumpled and folded. The colliding continents slowly pushed up, eventually creating Earth's great mountains.

There was one major problem with Wegener's idea. It didn't explain what pulled the continents apart. Because he couldn't pinpoint the cause of continental drift, other scientists did not accept his ideas. It would take scientists another 50 years to figure out exactly why continental drift occurs.

The Missing Piece of the Puzzle

By the late 1950s and early 1960s, scientists had tools to help them investigate the structure of the deep ocean floor. They saw a part of the ocean floor they called the mid-ocean ridge. This underwater mountain range helped them

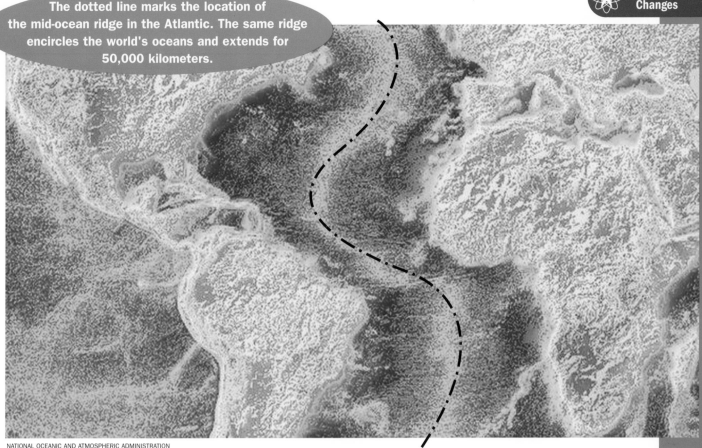

The dotted line marks the location of the mid-ocean ridge in the Atlantic. The same ridge encircles the world's oceans and extends for 50,000 kilometers.

NATIONAL OCEANIC AND ATMOSPHERIC ADMINISTRATION

understand how new ocean crust formed, and helped explain how the continents moved apart.

The discovery of the mid-ocean ridge made other scientists curious. They wanted to know what the ridge was and how it formed. An American geologist named Harry Hess studied maps of the mid-ocean ridge very carefully. He also noticed that new material is constantly being added to the ocean floor at the crest of the mid-ocean ridge. He revisited Wegener's idea that the continents move. After considering all the evidence, he supported Wegener's conclusion. Maybe the continents do move.

By the late 1960s, scientists developed a new theory about Earth. A theory is a well-tested idea that explains many different observations. This theory stated that the continental and oceanic crusts could be thought of as rigid plates that moved across Earth's surface.

These plates are in constant slow motion because of thermal currents moving inside Earth. The continental plates riding on the currents cause continents to drift and mountains to form. This idea came to be known as the theory of plate tectonics.

This theory was a major breakthrough. For many years, scientists had suspected that the surface of the Earth was always moving. They just couldn't explain why. As a result of the thinking of many different scientists over a long period of time, an innovative theory emerged. This theory also helps explain why earthquakes take place. The next story explains how knowledge of Earth's moving plates contributes to our understanding of earthquakes. ■

Something's

The aftermath of the
1995 earthquake in
Kobe, Japan

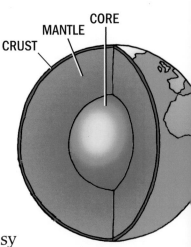

Earth's three main part
are like the layers of
hard-boiled egg

On January 17, 1995, one of the worst earthquakes in years struck the city of Kobe in Japan. Smoke smothered the city, and buildings toppled like toothpicks. Five thousand people lost their lives. What caused this terrible natural disaster? There are no easy explanations for earthquakes. To understand what causes earthquakes, it's important to first understand the structure of Earth.

Shaking

Let's begin with imagining Earth as a hard-boiled egg. The eggshell is Earth's crust. That's the part we live on and what represents the plates in the plate tectonic theory. The cooked egg white represents the mantle. The yolk is Earth's core.

The crust is not just one piece. It is split into about 20 pieces, much like the cracked shell on a hard-boiled egg. The pieces of shell are called plates. These plates are constantly moving because of thermal currents created by heat rising up from Earth's hot molten core.

At their boundaries, the plates constantly move against each other. These movements create friction, stress, and strain. Stress builds up. When the stress gets too great, the crust ruptures, and the plates slide past each other. Crash! Shock waves go out in all directions, like ripples on a pond. It is these waves that cause the rumbling and shaking of an earthquake.

Where Do Earthquakes Happen?

Earthquakes happen all over the world, but they are most common in certain places. The map below shows where those places are. What's interesting is that the earthquake zones outline the boundaries of Earth's major plates. That's not a coincidence. Earthquakes happen in places where the plates meet.

Regions of Major Earthquake Activity

One of the world's major earthquake concentrations extends around the Pacific Ocean. It is known as the Ring of Fire. About 80 percent of the world's largest earthquakes and volcanic eruptions occur here. A second big earthquake area extends from the east end of the Atlantic Ocean through the Mediterranean Sea.

The discovery of Earth's plates proved to be a major finding in two ways. First, it provided the explanation behind why continents drift apart. Second, moving plates and their interactions also helped explain why earthquakes occur. As long as the crustal plates that form Earth's continents continue to move, our planet will continue to change. ■

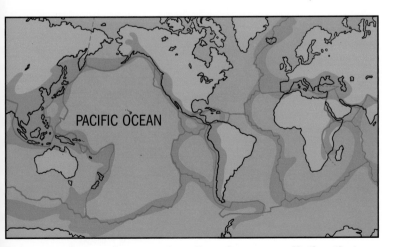

PACIFIC OCEAN

This map shows where most earthquakes occur. Notice that they are concentrated along the boundaries where Earth's crustal plates interact.

Volcano in a Cornfield

Dionisio Pulido was a farmer who lived in the middle of the 1900s. His farm was located in the small town of Paricutín, Mexico.

Pulido's farm had one unusual characteristic. There was always a small depression in his cornfield. Pulido and his wife had tried many times to fill the depression, but it always came back. In fact, a neighbor remembered playing near that depression as a child. He remembered hearing noises underground and feeling warmth coming from there.

One day in February 1943, Pulido got on his horse to go to his fields. He wanted to check on the spring planting. There was nothing unusual about this day, except for reports about earthquakes. But earthquakes were common in these parts. No one was too concerned.

Then something happened that changed everything. "I heard a noise like thunder, but I could not explain it, for the sky above was clear and the day was so peaceful," Pulido remembered.

Here is the place where Pulido first saw steam and ash erupting from the Earth on February 20, 1943. It didn't take long for the people of Paricutín to realize that a volcano was forming in the field.

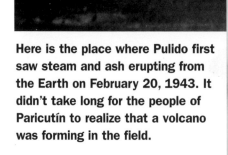

Dionisio Pulido

Then Pulido noticed something unusual. The depression in his field got deeper and wider. A few minutes later, he heard thunder again. The trees began to tremble. The ground around the depression rose into a mound about 2 meters (over 6 feet) high. Steam and fine dust began to blow up out of a vent in the center of the mound. The steam kept coming, and the noises got louder and louder.

Pulido was terrified. He couldn't imagine what was happening. He raced back to Paricutín and reported what he had seen and heard to the police.

What the Depression Was

By the next day, it was obvious what the depression was. It was a volcano! The volcano was ejecting rocks and steam. It kept getting bigger and bigger. By the fourth day, the volcano had risen to a height of 60 meters (196 feet). On the sixth day, it was 120 meters (394 feet). By the end of the first month, the volcano was 148 meters (485 feet) tall.

Many people traveled to Paricutín to watch the volcano grow. Tourists came to see what all the fuss was about. Reporters wrote articles about it. Geologists were fascinated. They just wanted to see what would happen next.

They soon found out. By the end of the first year, the volcano had grown to 336 meters (1,102 feet). Then its growth slowed down. ▸

SMITHSONIAN INSTITUTION ARCHIVES, RECORD UNIT 7281, WILLIAM F. FOSHAG COLLECTION, NEG. #98-3307

The ground around the depression rose into a mound about 2 meters (over 6 feet) high. Steam and fine dust began to blow up out of a vent in the center of the mound. After 1 month, the volcano was 148 meters (485 feet) tall.

The volcano after eight days of activity, February 28, 1943

Effects of the Volcano

The volcano's size was not the real problem. The ash and lava that poured out were much worse. Soon, ash fell on the ground, covering the town and its surrounding farms. When the rains came, the falling ash turned to streams of mud. The farms were ruined.

Then the lava started flowing. It covered the fields and approached the town. By June, it was clear what had to be done. Everyone, including Pulido, had to leave Paricutín.

SMITHSONIAN INSTITUTION ARCHIVES, RECORD UNIT 7281, WILLIAM F. FOSHAG COLLECTION. TOP (NEG. #98-3304) BOTTOM (NEG. #98-3305)

The volcano in January 1944. Ash covered the fields.

Today, Paricutín and much of the nearby countryside is silent. No one lives there anymore. The town is buried under lava. ■

The volcano forced the people of Paricutín to leave their homes.

ROCKS IN OUR WORLD

THE ROCKS THAT OCCUR AT THE SURFACE OF THE EARTH ARE FORMED BY A VARIETY OF PROCESSES. PEOPLE HAVE LONG KNOWN HOW TO DIG UP THOSE ROCKS AND USE THEM IN BUILDINGS. IN FACT, IF YOU LOOK AT SOME BUILDINGS, YOU CAN FIGURE OUT WHAT KIND OF ROCK THEY ARE MADE FROM.

Sonya Berger, a park ranger with the National Park Service in Washington, D.C., has developed a different kind of tour of our capitol's famous monuments. She shows visitors the rocks that were used to build each monument.

Before you travel along with Sonya, let's look at the three main kinds of rocks: igneous, sedimentary, and metamorphic. Each is formed in a different way.

IGNEOUS ROCKS form when hot melted rocks deep inside Earth, called magma, cool and solidify. Granite is an example of an igneous rock. Granite is very strong and chemically resistant and makes an excellent building material. A piece of granite is made up of different mineral grains that vary in color. You can find white, pink, gray and black minerals. The mineral grains make the granite sparkle.

SEDIMENTARY ROCKS form from different materials, such as sand, mud, and pebbles, or the remains of animals and plants. Such materials are called sediment. That's where the name of this type of rock comes from. Over millions of years, these soft sediments are pressed together by the load of overlying sediments to form hard rocks. As new sediment falls on top of the old sediment, new layers form. Natural cements fill in the spaces between the sediment. After millions of years, the mineral grains and tiny rock fragments harden to form sedimentary rocks. Limestone is a sedimentary rock.

METAMORPHIC ROCKS are those that have changed over long periods of time. Metamorphic rocks were once igneous or sedimentary rocks. They were changed over time by intense heat and pressure when they were buried deep inside Earth's surface. Marble is an example of metamorphic rock. It changed from limestone, a sedimentary rock. ▶

THEY (WHO) SEEK TO ESTABLISH SYSTEMS OF GOVERNMENT BASED ON THE REGIMENTATION OF ALL HUMAN BEINGS BY A HANDFUL OF INDIVIDUAL RULERS... CALL THIS A NEW ORDER. IT IS NOT NEW AND IT IS NOT ORDER.

This is a statue of FDR with his faithful dog, Fala. FDR was president of the United States during the Great Depression and World War II.

TERRY J. ADAMS, NATIONAL PARK SERVICE

Rocks as Building Materials

Now that you know a little bit about different kinds of rocks, it's time to take a tour of Washington, D.C. We'll stop at famous buildings and monuments in the city and find out what kind of rocks they are made of. Sonya will be our guide.

▲ **"THE FIRST STOP IS THE FRANKLIN DELANO ROOSEVELT (FDR) MEMORIAL,"** says Sonya. FDR was president of the United States during the Great Depression and World War II, in the 1930s and 1940s. During those years, people faced many difficulties. Many people didn't have jobs or enough money for food. During the war, many people had to fight. FDR had to help bring the citizens of the United States together to overcome their difficulties. That's why many people believe it's fitting that his memorial is made of granite. Granite is very strong,

and symbolizes FDR's leadership skills as he guided the country through troublesome times.

▼ **"NEXT, LET'S TRAVEL TO THE WHITE HOUSE,"** Sonya continues. "The White House is made from sandstone, a sedimentary rock. Builders brought the sandstone to the city from Virginia."

But this sandstone was not very strong. Even after many repairs, some stones have had to be replaced. Between 1980 and 1997, workers rebuilt parts of the White House with leftover sandstone from part of the Capitol Building. Because the natural color of sandstone is tan and not white, the building had to be painted. Otherwise, the White House would have to be called the Tan House.

The White House as it looks today.

Wouldn't you know it? We're just in time to see Abraham Lincoln take a shower!

▲ **"NEXT, LET'S GO TO THE LINCOLN MEMORIAL,"** says Sonya. "This famous monument is made from all three types of rocks." The steps are made of igneous granite. The statute of Abraham Lincoln is carved from metamorphic marble. The walls and columns surrounding Lincoln are made of sedimentary limestone.

Lincoln was president during the Civil War, a time when the country was divided. He worked very hard to bring the country back together. Maybe that's why all three types of rocks are used in his memorial. They represent Lincoln's life-long goal of trying to unite our country. What's more, these rocks come from six different states located in both the northern and southern parts of the country.

▶ **NO TRIP TO WASHINGTON, D.C., WOULD BE COMPLETE WITHOUT A VISIT TO THE WASHINGTON MONUMENT.** That's where Sonya ends her tour. You can see a photograph of the Washington Monument on the next page. The outside of this majestic building is made of marble. To make sure the building was strong enough to support its height, builders used granite inside. The granite gives the tall building extra support.

There is another surprise behind the plain white marble of the Washington Monument. Inside its walls are 193 stones from all over the world. This collection of stones includes different rocks from different parts of the United States.

The tour of monuments in Washington, D.C., is now over. Ranger Sonya hopes you enjoyed your visit. As you now ▶

know, there is more to each monument than meets the eye. Each one makes the best possible use of rocks, Earth's building blocks.

Rocks are important building materials. Often you can figure out what kind of rock was used for construction. Look around the place where you live. Pay attention to the different buildings. Can you tell which rocks were used? ■

The tall, white Washington Monument stands out against the pink sky. Without the tough granite inside, this building would not be as sturdy as it is.

PART 1 CONCLUSION

How Earth Changes

THAT'S A FACT!   Alfred Wegener was the first scientist to suggest that Earth's continents are always moving. Over a period of about 50 years, other scientists added to his thoughts and developed the theory of plate tectonics.

I KNOW THAT ONE!   How did the theory of plate tectonics change the way people looked at the world?

FIGURE IT OUT!   What is the relationship between Pangaea and a building toppled by an earthquake?

HERE'S ONE MORE!   What are the three main types of rocks on Earth? What are the different processes that form each type?

The Search for Water

You will read the following stories in Part 2:
- **Where Does Our Drinking Water Come From?**
- **Drilling for Water**
- **Chinese River Painting**
- **Water Scientist**
- **The Dust Bowl**

What ties these stories together is water. Water is a unique and interesting substance. Take a look at the Cool Water Facts in the bubbles to find out why.

In this section, you'll find out how engineers search for water underground and how they figure out how to get water to people and the places where they live. And you'll meet different scientists who study water and learn what they have discovered. You'll read, too, how knowledge about soil saved the Great Plains.

Water also inspires people to write poetry and create beautiful paintings. In this section, you will see how people from one part of the world expressed their feelings about water.

Cool Water Facts

Three-quarters of Earth's surface is covered by water.

Our bodies are composed of two-thirds water.

Humans can live for days on nothing but water.

Where Does Our Drinking Water Come From?

How many ways do you use water? Washing your hands is one way, and so is drinking water. And there's nothing like a dip in the swimming pool on a hot summer day. Did you know that each person in the United States uses an average of 350 liters of water (about 93 gallons) each day?

NSRC

MOST OF THE WATER ON EARTH IS FOUND IN OCEANS. BUT WE CAN'T DRINK THIS WATER. DO YOU KNOW WHY? Ocean water is very salty. It tastes awful, and drinking too much could lead to dehydration. There are ways to remove the salt from the water, but these techniques are expensive. They also take a long time. So using ocean water as drinking water is not done much, at least not right now.

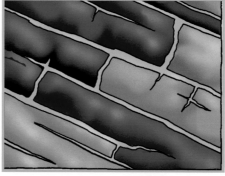

Groundwater moves through cracks like these.

WHAT WE NEED IS FRESH WATER. Some fresh water comes from lakes and streams. These sources are called surface waters. Other fresh water is hidden underground. This kind of fresh water is called groundwater.

Groundwater is water that has fallen to the earth as rain or snow. It seeps through layers of sand, gravel, and rocks located underground. ▶

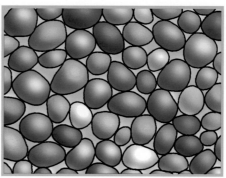

Groundwater settles in spaces between rocks.

The water settles between spaces in the rocks. Underground rock formations that contain water are called aquifers.

Aquifers

Aquifers are found at different depths beneath Earth's surface. Some are found just below the surface. Others are hundreds of meters down. But people rarely find aquifers below 2,500 feet (800 meters). That's because the weight of the rocks below this level is so great that most of the cracks and spaces close up. Then there's no room for water.

Two Different Kinds of Aquifers

Look at these two pictures. They show two different kinds of aquifers. Most aquifers look like the one on the right. The water can flow freely. The top layer of the aquifer is called the water table. The water table is ground-

water closest to the surface of the ground. The middle layer is permeable; water can flow freely through here. The bottom layer is impermeable; water cannot flow through this layer.

The second kind of aquifer, shown at the bottom of the page, is a whole different story. It's surrounded by rock that water can't pass through. That means that the water is trapped, or confined. When a well is drilled into a confined aquifer, the water flows to the surface like a fountain. This kind of aquifer is called an artesian aquifer.

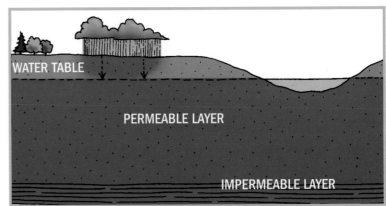

The water in this aquifer can flow freely through the permeable layer.

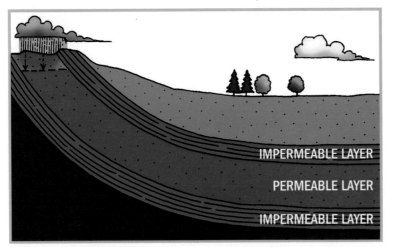

The water in this aquifer is trapped. Water can't pass through the surrounding rock.

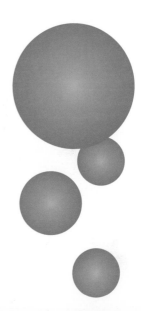

PHOTO BY GEOFFREY DE VERTEUIL, 1996

Bustling cities like Los Angeles get their water from rivers hundreds of miles away.

How Do We Get Our Water?

If you live in a city or town, you probably get your water from a public utility company. Utility companies pump water to your home either from surface waters or from aquifers.

Sometimes utility companies must send the water from lakes or rivers through pipes for hundreds of miles. The pipes that bring water to a big city may be so large that you could stand in them. Water tunnels in New York City are so large you could drive a truck through them!

If you live far from a city, you probably get your water from a well drilled in the ground. Well drillers are workers who drill holes deep into the ground to find out how deep the groundwater is. ▶

Sometimes a well can be more than 300 meters (984 feet) deep! After the well is drilled, the driller puts a plastic or steel pipe that looks like a giant drinking straw into the hole. This keeps the soil and rock from caving in. Then the well driller lowers a pump into the hole. The pump forces the water that has seeped into the pipe upward, through a pipe, and into your house.

Cleaning the Water

Have you ever poured sandy water through a strainer at the beach? The strainer is a filter. It separates some of the sand from the water. You might say it helps to clean the water.

The land can be a filter, too. As water seeps through the soil, layers of sand and gravel clean the water. Spring water is underground water that bubbles to the surface. It has been filtered by the land. That's why people can often drink it just the way it is.

Surface waters, however, usually are not clean. As water flows over land, it wears away soil and rock and carries the particles along. This is called erosion. Pollutants—like fertilizer, road salt and other chemicals, and bacteria—can get into both

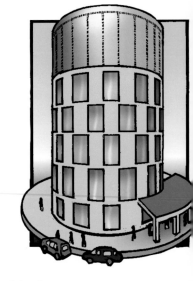

surface water and groundwater. Then the water is not safe to drink.

Utility companies must clean the water before people can use it. In treatment plants, utility companies add certain chemicals to the water. For example, chlorine gets rid of bacteria that might harm you. Alum makes particles clump together and sink.

After the sediment is removed, the water is passed through layers of sand and gravel. These layers filter the water and remove smaller particles. This is called filtration. Before the water can be stored or distributed to homes and businesses, utility plant workers bubble air through the water to make it taste fresh. Many utility companies add fluoride to the water, too. This helps keep your teeth from getting cavities.

Getting the Clean Water to You

After the water has been cleaned, it goes to a water tower. Utility companies use water towers to store clean water until you are ready to use it.

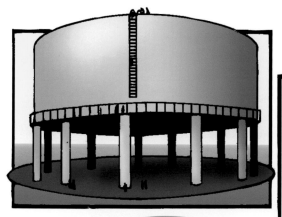

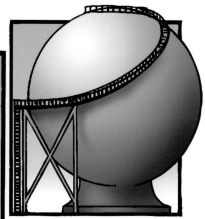

Although these water towers look different, they are all quite tall. There's a reason for that. When water is released from a tall structure, the pressure from the water pushes it down and through the pipes that carry it to homes and businesses.

Why do you think water towers are so tall? That is because the water pressure is greater when the column of water falls from a greater height. When water is released from the tower, the pressure of the water pushes it down and through pipes. The pipes carry the water directly to your home, offices, and other buildings.

Water travels on a long journey from its source to our homes. In the process, it is cleaned so that it is safe. So the next time you see water disappear down the drain, think about where it has to go before we can use it again. ■

COURTESY OF WEEKS DRILLING AND PUMP CO.

Don Garner is an expert on drilling for water.

DRILLING

WHEN SOMEONE WANTS A WELL DRILLED, THE FIRST QUESTION WELL DRILLERS ASK IS, "HOW FAR BELOW THE SURFACE OF THE LAND IS THE GROUND-WATER?" ONCE THEY KNOW THIS, THEY CAN FIGURE OUT HOW MUCH WATER IS AVAILABLE.

DRILLING FOR WATER IS AN IMPORTANT JOB. THERE ARE MANY COMPANIES THAT SPECIALIZE IN IT. THE WEEKS DRILLING AND PUMP COMPANY IN SONOMA COUNTY, CALIFORNIA, IS ONE OF THOSE COMPANIES. THEY HAVE BEEN IN THE BUSINESS OF LOCATING AND DRILLING WELLS SINCE 1951. THEY HAVE A PRETTY GOOD IDEA OF WHAT IT TAKES TO BE SUCCESSFUL.

DON GARNER WORKS FOR WEEKS DRILLING. HE EXPLAINS WHAT DRILLING IS LIKE.

for WATER

Figuring Out Where the Water Is

"The first step," says Don, "is to go to the files." That means that he has to find out about other wells his company has dug. The company has dug quite a few—about 20,000 in all. It has information in files about all of these wells. Engineers from the company know where they've been successful at finding water and where they haven't. There also is a lot of information about many underground rock formations that contain water.

But sometimes Weeks Drilling goes to an area about which it has little information. In those cases, Don says, he looks closely at the geology of the land. ▶

COURTESY OF WEEKS DRILLING AND PUMP CO.

When the company drilled through the top layer, the pressure in the artesian aquifer forced the underground water up quickly.

Whoosh!

He knows that some spots, such as valleys or areas part way up a mountain, are more likely to have water.

Careful Planning...

Deciding on the best place to dig involves careful planning. For example, the location has to follow laws about drilling. Wells must be 30 meters (98 feet) or more from a sewer system. They also can't be too close to someone's house or business. The drillers have to be able to get the drilling rig to the site. That's not always easy. Rigs are enormous!

Don says that in California, it's hard to predict where you're going to find water. "You may not find water in one spot, then unexpectedly you'll find it close by," Don explains.

...But Still Surprises

"Each well can be a new discovery. You never exactly know what will happen," says Don. Recently, the company was drilling some wells for new houses. The first one didn't produce as much water as was needed. So the workers drilled the next one 15 meters (50 feet) deeper. They were in for a surprise. They had struck an artesian aquifer. The water in an artesian aquifer is trapped between two

COURTESY OF WEEKS DRILLING AND PUMP CO.

Weeks Drilling has been finding good water 95 percent of the time for quite a while. ■

Drilling for water

COURTESY OF WEEKS DRILLING AND PUMP CO.

waterproof rock layers. When the company drilled through the top layer, the pressure in the aquifer forced the underground water up quickly. Whoosh!

"It was spurting up in the air, putting out water at 750 gallons a minute," explains Don.

Don says that the part of his job that he doesn't like is "when I have to deliver bad news to people. Tell them that we had no success—that we struck a dry well." Fortunately, that doesn't happen very often.

Success! The drillers found water.

Chinese River Painting

FREER GALLERY OF ART, SMITHSONIAN INSTITUTION, WASHINGTON, D.C.: PURCHASE, F1930.80

A hand scroll is a painting done on a long strip of paper or silk. The strip is then rolled up. To view the scroll, you unroll it section by section—to see its story unfold.

Rivers are frequently a main feature of hand scrolls. That's because they are an important part of the landscape. People admired the beauty of rivers and depended on them for food, transportation, and water.

Fishermen on a River

The picture above, called *Fishermen on an Autumn River,* is a section of a hand scroll that was painted about 600 years ago in China. The scroll tells a story about life on the river. This section gives a glimpse into the daily lives of fishermen and their families.

This painter thought that river people had a romantic life filled with freedom and harmony. The river is calm in the picture. Fishermen and their families are taking a break from work. The boats are pulling together so that people can talk and relax. Can you find the group of men on the bank? They're having a picnic. Nearby, some children are playing.

See the pointed shapes at the bottom of the scroll? They are fishing nets drying in the sun. There's also a laundry line with clothes hanging out to dry. It's tucked between the trees.

Rapids on the Yangtze River

Shooting the Rapids

Here's a section of another Chinese hand scroll, called *Rapids on the Yangtze River.* The Yangtze is China's mightiest river.

The view here shows a passenger boat that has just emerged from a narrow gorge. Now it is rushing down the rapids. The man in the back part of the boat has his hands on the rudder. He's struggling to steer and keep the boat under control. The boatman in the front is using a long pole to avoid dangerous rocks.

Look closely inside the cabin of the boat. You can see the faces of passengers peering out. What do you think they are feeling as they zoom down the rapids?

Rivers Inspire Poems

The upper Yangtze River has many rapids. Some shoot through gorges. The rapids have inspired many poems. Here's one by the poet Su Shi, who lived from 1037 to 1101.

ON THE RIVER, VIEWING THE MOUNTAINS

From my boat I watch the hills race by like horses,

All at once a herd of several hundred flashes past,

Hills in front, hacked and jagged, fast changing,

Ranges behind, all a-jumble, bolting off in fright.

Looking up, I see a faint track zigzag round-about,

Someone is walking high upon it, dim and indistinct.

On the boat I wave my hand, wishing to have a chat,

But my lonely sail flies south like a soaring bird.

(Translation—Stephen D. Allee)

What do you think the poem is about? What is the poet saying about the land? What do you think he is saying about the water? Could you write a poem about a river near you? ■

The farm where Karen grew up proved to be fertile ground for her first big research project.

WATER SCIENTIST

WHEN KAREN PRESTEGAARD WAS A **LITTLE GIRL,** she loved to sit on a hill on her family's farm. She lived in Soldier's Grove, Wisconsin, near the Kickapoo River. Karen used to watch the river flood each spring. She wondered what caused the floods. She thought about how the land was worn down, or eroded, after each flood. She used to imagine how the flowing water would change the land over time.

In 1989, Karen returned to her farm as a scientist to answer those questions. Her family's farm was the first place she studied. Her goal was to study how a dam built in the 1970s had affected the plants and animals living along the river.

WHAT KIND OF SCIENTIST IS KAREN? She describes herself as both a hydrologist and a geomorphologist. "Hydro" means water; hydrologists are scientists who study water. "Geo" means land and "morph" means form or shape. Geomorphologists study how Earth's landforms change. Karen is interested in how water changes the land. ▶

Karen wades into her work.

Land and Water Research

Karen's work on her family farm was just the beginning. Since then, she has done research on land and water in different places around the country. She has studied marshes in Maryland and mountain streams in Montana. Often, she works with her students and other researchers.

At each spot, Karen and her team have a different problem to solve. In Montana, Karen is interested in how streams flowing through the mountains erode the land and carry soil and gravel from the mountains to the plains. In Maryland, the researchers are trying to understand why there is so much algae in the water. Too much algae can cause plants in the water to die. Then the animals that eat those plants don't have enough food.

Field Work

Karen looks at many different parts of the streams she studies. She asks the following questions:

1 How fast does the water flow?

2 How much water is in the stream?

3 What is in the water?

How Fast Does the Water Flow?

As part of Karen's study in Maryland, she measures how fast the stream is flowing. She calculates how much water passes through the stream in a given amount of time— the flow rate. She measures the flow rates in different parts of the stream.

Karen takes measurements of the size and shape of the stream and then calculates how much water passes through the stream.

How Much Water Is in the Stream?

Researchers also need to know how much water is in the stream. First, they use surveying equipment to find out the size and shape of the stream. Then they can figure out about how much water can fit in that space.

What Is in the Water?

To learn more about the water, researchers collect water samples. They set up a small box at the bottom of the stream. The box fills with water and other materials. The scientists use clean plastic bottles to scoop up samples from the box.

Back at the Lab

Karen and her team bring the samples back to their lab. They run the samples though a filter, and they weigh the sediment that filters out. Next, they compare the weight of sediment with the weight of water in the sample. From this work, they can tell how much sediment the stream was carrying at that time. The last thing they do is analyze the filtered water. They are interested in finding out what chemicals are in the water. This information tells the scientists how clean the water is. It also provides some information about the history of the stream.

Is being a hydrologist hard work?

Absolutely! But Karen loves it.

She likes being outside and getting exercise. She likes using her brain to solve problems. Most of all, she loves the water. ■

KAREN PRESTEGAARD, UNIVERSITY OF MARYLAND, COLLEGE PARK

The water samples will give Karen and her team key information about the water in the stream. They will be able to determine how much sediment was in the water as well as how many chemicals it was carrying.

The Dust Bowl

WHERE DO YOU THINK THIS PICTURE WAS TAKEN? Believe it or not, it is the Great Plains of the United States. The Great Plains are supposed to be green. This land is where wheat is grown.

Drought and Black Blizzards

Back in 1931, parts of the Great Plains looked like this photograph. A terrible drought had set in. The drought caused the land to dry up. Dust storms—whirlwinds of dense, powdery dust clouds—began blowing across the flat, treeless countryside. These storms were called black blizzards.

The dust was once topsoil held to the ground by prairie grasses that stretched as far as the eye could see. Farmers didn't realize that the strong roots of these grasses protected the precious topsoil. They plowed the grasses away and planted wheat and corn on almost every square inch of the plain.

When the drought came, the wheat shriveled and died. Wheat does not have strong roots like prairie grasses do. So when the wheat died, there was little to hold the soil to the land. As the harsh prairie wind blew, black dust clouds swept across the dry fields and into towns, homes, and schools.

Hugh Bennett gazes at the dusty surface of the Great Plains.

Wind carried away the fertile soil. Farmers could no longer grow crops here.

Saving the Farms

Hugh Bennett was a scientist who specialized in studying soil. He grew up on a cotton farm in North Carolina. He knew a lot about agriculture and wanted to help save the land. Bennett went to Washington, D.C., and talked to President Franklin D. Roosevelt and the U.S. Congress about a new approach to farming. He convinced them that a special agency was needed to help protect the soil and the land. This agency was called the Soil Conservation Service.

The people who lived in this region began to lose hope for the future. Many people—one out of four—packed up a few belongings and left their homes and neighbors behind. During this period, the southern Great Plains came to be known as the Dust Bowl. The Dust Bowl lasted for almost 10 years. Then help finally came to the people who lived there.

Protecting the Soil

Agents from the Soil Conservation Service showed farmers new ways to farm the land. The agents helped the farmers understand why they should save the soil. Farmers learned to plant a line of trees, called windbreaks, around their fields. The trees helped block the wind. Farmers also began plowing their fields by following the ▶

NATIONAL ARCHIVES AND RECORDS ADMINISTRATION

Planting crops in patterns like these helped the soil hold in precious water.

contours of the land. These patterns helped the soil hold in rainwater. Finally, farmers built reservoirs that held large amounts of water. The water in the reservoirs was used to irrigate the fields and provide water for cattle.

Farmers were paid to use the new planting and plowing methods— and to grow fewer crops. They also rotated the kinds of crops they planted. One year, they planted crops such as wheat, which took many nutrients from the soil. The next year, they planted crops such as soybeans, which put nutrients back into the soil.

At first, the farmers didn't want to make these changes. But over time, they began to understand why they had to work their fields in new ways. The land had its limits. It had to be cared for so it would not be overworked again.

It took about three years for these changes to make a difference. Most of the soil stayed on the ground during the last days of the drought. At the end of the summer of 1939, the rains fell again on the southern plains. Over time, the land was restored. ■

PART 2 CONCLUSION

The Search for Water

THAT'S A FACT!   Three-quarters of Earth is covered by water, but most of this is saltwater and not suitable for drinking.

THAT'S EASY!   What do hydrologists study? Why is their research important?

WHAT DO YOU THINK?   What caused the Dust Bowl? What strategies did farmers learn to prevent another one from taking place?

PART 3

Exploring Land and Water

We live on the land, and we depend on water to survive. The land and the water are essential to life on Earth.

You will read the following seven stories in Part 3:

- Journeying Down the Grand Canyon
- Painter of the Land
- Adventure in a Cave
- Glaciers: Rivers of Ice
- Satellites: New Tools for New Explorations
- Joseph Henry: The Father of Weather Forecasting
- What's the Forecast?

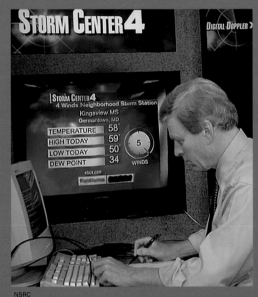

NSRC

These stories focus on explorers of the land and water. Some of these explorers set out long ago to learn more about our landscape. Other explorers are working now, investigating small sections of our planet.

Some explorers don't go out into the wild. They learn about the land and the water—and how they are connected—by gathering information from different kinds of instruments. These explorers are meteorologists, scientists who study the weather. In this section, you will find out about the history of weather forecasting and the tools meteorologists use today.

Journeying Down the
GRAND CANYON

ANYON NATIONAL PARK, NATIONAL PARK SERVICE

THE GRAND CANYON IN ARIZONA IS ONE OF THE WONDERS OF THE WORLD. But it wasn't explored until 1869. In fact, maps in the 1860s showed the canyon and surrounding territory as a 4,931-square kilometer (1,904-square mile) blank space with a label: "Unexplored."

Then Major John Wesley Powell came along and changed that label. A curious and determined man, he set out to explore the canyon. Even though he had lost part of his right arm in the Civil War, he had made up his mind. He was going to travel through the Grand Canyon. ▸

Hikers stop to admire the Grand Canyon. Do you see the layers of rock in the formations in the distance? Each layer is unique and formed at a different time. Together, the layers tell a story about the history of the Grand Canyon.

Major John Wesley Powell in 1869

A Small Group Prepares

Powell was a self-taught scientist who had some experience navigating rivers. He understood how important it was to prepare thoroughly for his trip. Before setting out, Powell gathered information about the area. He also talked with Indians, settlers, and trappers. They had all spent time near the canyon.

Powell designed a special wooden rowboat for the journey. Then he had four boats built. He convinced nine volunteers to accompany him. They brought along supplies for 10 months. They also brought a compass, to help them find their way.

On May 24, 1869, Powell and his volunteers launched the boats into the Green River, the main tributary, or branch, of the Colorado River. Their goal was to explore the canyons of both rivers.

Powell's boa in water the Gra Cany

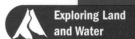
The Trip Begins

On May 27, the party arrived at its first canyon on the Green River. The travelers encountered walls 360 meters (1,181 feet) high towering above them. Soon the men came across rapids and waterfalls. When the falls were too steep, the men rowed to shore. They emptied the boats of cargo, attached ropes to the front and back ends of the boats, and lowered them over. They called this method "lining." The men carried their supplies on land, next to the boats.

ese wooden boats would
rry explorers on the
venture of their lives.

STATES GEOLOGICAL SURVEY PHOTO ARCHIVE

Day after day, wet, scratched, and sunburned, the men battled the river. On June 10, they lost a boat over a waterfall. On June 16, their campfire flared up. Clothing and supplies were lost in the flames. ▸

Lining the boats, or gently lowering them over the falls.

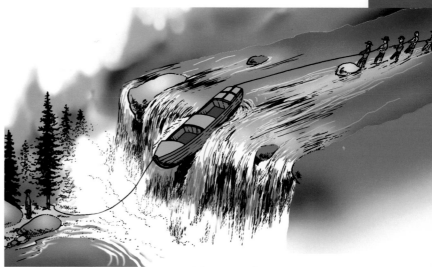

Powell stops to talk to an American Indian near the Grand Canyon prior to the boat trip.

Into the Unknown

On July 6, the party entered uncharted territory, a canyon that was so barren that they later named it *Desolation*. Day after day, the men navigated through dangerous rapids.

After a week, the river slowed. On July 17, with no clue except for increased water speed, the Green River joined the Colorado. Two months and 861 kilometers (535 miles) had passed to get them to this point. Their food supply would last only two more months. Could they make it?

The Canyon at Last

After a last flurry of rapids, the Colorado River started to run straight and fast. They were able to cover 20 miles a day.

On August 10, they arrived at the foot of the Grand Canyon. Powell wrote, "We are three quarters of a mile in the depths of the earth. We have an unknown distance yet to run; an unknown river yet to explore."

By now, the men were tired and overworked. Much of their food had spoiled. The canyon walls were so narrow that the men slept on rocks at night. On August 27, with only five days of supplies left, they met the most dangerous falls of all. Three men refused to go farther.

But Powell and six others pushed on. The next day, they left one leaky boat behind, fired up their courage, and ran the falls with the remaining boats. Just as they finished those falls, they unexpectedly came upon another set of falls—it was too close to avoid. They went over. Against all odds, they survived.

On August 29, the two boats descended out of the Grand Canyon, drifting into a large valley. "Now the danger is over," Powell wrote. "The river rolls by us in silent majesty; the quiet of the camp is sweet; our joy is almost ecstasy." Powell had accomplished his goal. He put the Grand Canyon on the map.

By opening up the Grand Canyon and the Colorado River, Powell made it possible for other explorers to develop a deeper understanding of the geology of the region. ■

Painter of the Land

THOMAS MORAN, *GRAND CANYON OF THE YELLOWSTONE*, 1872, OIL ON CANVAS, THE U.S. DEPARTMENT OF THE INTERIOR MUSEUM, WASHINGTON, D.C.

This is a painting of the Yellowstone Falls in Yellowstone National Park. It was painted by an artist named Thomas Moran. Moran lived in Philadelphia in the 1800s. Even though he was from a city on the East Coast, he loved the West. Its wild landscape amazed him. Moran returned to the West many times throughout his life to sketch new landscapes for his paintings.

Do you know how big this painting is? It's huge—7 feet tall and 12 feet wide. Moran was trying to capture the splendor of Yellowstone in his painting. Do you think he succeeded?

Traveling West

How did Moran get to Yellowstone? Remember, in the 1800s, it wasn't so easy to travel west. Moran got there by joining a group sponsored by the government. Members of the group were surveying the land. While others were measuring the land, Moran spent his time making watercolor sketches of geysers, waterfalls, and mountain cliffs. He used these sketches to compose the huge oil painting of Yellowstone.

The painting turned out to be more than just a fabulous piece of art. It became evidence that ▸

Yellowstone was worth preserving. The leader of the surveying trip, F.V. Hayden, borrowed Moran's painting and showed it to members of Congress. He thought the painting captured the magnificence of Yellowstone. Hayden turned out to be right. In March 1872, Congress made Yellowstone the first national park in the United States. In June, Congress purchased Moran's painting for $10,000. It was the first landscape painting to hang in the U.S. Capitol.

YELLOWSTONE NATIONAL PARK, NATIONAL PARK SERVICE

A Life of Landscapes

What happened to Thomas Moran? He spent his life traveling and painting. His next adventure was a journey with John Wesley Powell to the Grand Canyon (see *Journeying Down the Grand Canyon*, page 41). This trip led to another huge painting, called the *Chasm of the Colorado*. Throughout his life, Moran painted many of America's most spectacular landscapes: the Colorado Rockies, the Grand Tetons in Wyoming, and the Shoshone Falls on the Snake River in Idaho.

At each place he visited, Moran always began drawing in the same way. First, he made watercolor sketches. He drew in the important forms, such as rocks and trees. Then he painted in some important colors and made notes about them. He used these sketches to create larger oil paintings when he arrived back home.

People called Moran the "dean of American landscape painters" and "the father of the national parks." But he called himself "TYM," or "Thomas 'Yellowstone' Moran." He wanted to keep that landscape a part of him. Yellowstone had a special place in his heart. ■

One of Moran's watercolor sketches used to make a painting

Adventure in a Cave

Did you ever wonder what exploring a cave is like? Just ask Tim Rose, a geologist at the Smithsonian Institution. In his spare time, Tim likes to explore a particular feature of the earth—caves.

Tim has been a spelunker, or cave explorer, for years. He's been inside more than 100 caves. Here, Tim is exploring a cave in Hawaii. ▶

a cave explorer is called a pelunker—funny name!

LET'S GO!

Preparing for the Trip

What clothes do cavers need to wear? What about gear? Here's what Tim and other spelunkers use to explore caves.

Warm Clothes and Coveralls

Tim wears warm clothes—plus coveralls. That's because it's cold and wet inside a cave. "The average temperature in most limestone caves is about 13 degrees Celsius (55 degrees Fahrenheit) all year long," says Tim. "And the humidity is about 100 percent. When you breathe out, you can see your breath." In some caves, there's so much cold water that people wear wet suits to stay warm.

Helmet

Tim wears a helmet to protect him from bumps and falling rocks.

Electric Lamp

Attached to the helmet is an electric lamp. It is Tim's most important piece of equipment. Most caves are totally dark. The only thing Tim can see is what his lamp shines on—the part of the cave directly in front of him.

Gloves and Kneepads

Tim pulls on tough gloves to protect his hands. He slips on a pair of kneepads because he will be spending a lot of time crawling to get through small passages and tunnels.

Backpack

Inside his backpack are a small first-aid kit, food, and drinks. Tim will spend several hours—maybe even half a day—inside the cave. He's sure to get hungry, so the food is necessary. And water is vital when his body is working so hard.

Buddies

The most important thing that Tim needs for caving isn't something he

Cavers spend a lot of time on their hands and knees, crawling around.

wears or carries in his backpack. It's his friends. The most important rule of caving is "Never cave alone."

"You need at least two buddies, and four is actually safer," Tim says. "If someone gets hurt, then one person can stay with him and two can go for help."

Entering the Cave

At the mouth of the cave, Tim and his buddies make sure their electric lamps are working. They also check to see if

Like any good scientist, Tim writes down what he observes.

they have extra batteries. They will be in the cave for a few hours. They have to be extra careful that they always have light handy. Cavers dread being in the dark!

As the cavers move along, they may find fossils, bones, or interesting rocks. Along the way, Tim makes notes about what he sees. But Tim and his pals never take anything from the cave, and they never leave anything behind. "Caves are nonrenewable natural resources," says Tim. "That means if they're destroyed, they're gone forever. Caves also have a unique geology and ecosystem. It's important not to disturb that."

If they're lucky, Tim and his friends may see a stalactite or a stalagmite. **STALACTITES** are long, thin deposits of a substance called calcium carbonate. They hang from the roof of a cave. Some are shaped like icicles. Others look like thin drinking straws. **STALAGMITES** are bumpy patches of calcium carbonate that form on the floor of a cave. They can grow quite tall. But these are not common features in caves. Mostly, the cavers do a lot of crawling and exploring—following interesting twists and turns.

There's always an exciting sense of discovery inside a cave. "I really feel like an explorer," says Tim. "I guess you could call caves one of Earth's last frontiers." ■

Glaciers: Rivers of Ice

DO YOU KNOW WHAT GLACIERS ARE? THEY ARE HUGE SHEETS OF MOVING ICE.

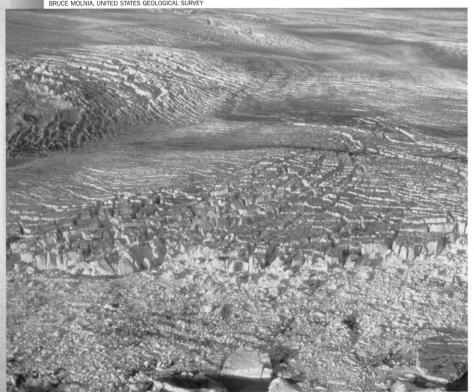

The Bering Glacier in Alaska

ALTHOUGH YOU CAN'T ALWAYS TELL THAT GLACIERS ARE MOVING, THEY ALWAYS ARE. Their own weight keeps them sliding downhill.

Believe it or not, glaciers cover about 10 percent of the land on Earth.

They also store about 75 percent of Earth's fresh water. In the United States, most of the glaciers are in Alaska. People in Washington state and Alaska get a lot of their water from glaciers.

Take a look at North America's largest glacier—the Bering Glacier. Located in Alaska, the Bering Glacier is the size of Rhode Island. That's one big glacier!

Like all glaciers, the Bering Glacier changes all the time. Bruce Molnia, a scientist at the U.S. Geological Survey (USGS), has been studying this glacier for years. Several years ago, the glacier began acting strangely. Here's what happened.

Unusual Behavior

In the spring of 1993, an Alaskan pilot, Gail Rainey, noticed something unusual. As she flew over the glacier on her weekly mail run, she saw that unusual lines and cracks had formed on the glacier's surface. Fortunately,

Bruce Molnia

(BOTH) BRUCE MOLNIA, UNITED STATES GEOLOGICAL SURVEY

Rainey was also a volunteer glacier watcher for the USGS. Gail picked up the phone and called Bruce Molnia in his Reston, Virginia, office. "Something odd is happening," she said.

Molnia was delighted to hear from Rainey. The odd behavior that she reported was not strange to Molnia. In fact, he had been expecting it for months. About every 30 years, cracks appear in the ice. The glacier gets thinner and longer. As the glacier stretches out, it moves forward. Geologists call this behavior a surge.

What Causes a Surge?

Surges take place after a glacier has been melting for a long time. As glaciers melt, a layer of water builds up under them. It takes quite a while for water to build up—about 30 years. When there is enough water under the glacier, changes take place. The glacier cracks and thins out. Water gathers at the bottom of the glacier. When this happens, the glacier starts skidding downhill, much like a car does on an icy road. Imagine an enormous sheet of ice gliding out of control down a mountain and you'll start to get the idea. ▶

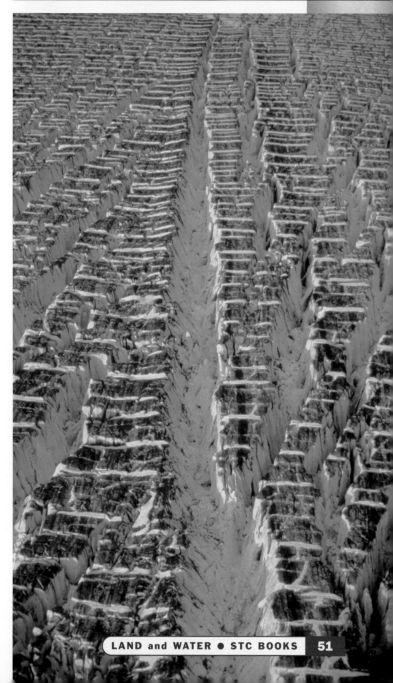

A close-up of the unusual lines and cracks in a surging glacier

Melting ice and water cause the glacier to move forward in fits and starts. That's when geologists know that a glacier is experiencing a surge.

A geologist pauses for a moment at the site of a surging glacier. She will soon explore the landscape, noting how the surging glacier changed it.

MOLNIA AND OTHER SCIENTISTS CONTINUE TO CHECK OUT THE BERING GLACIER. THEY WANT TO SEE HOW THE GLACIER CHANGED THE LANDSCAPE. THEY'RE ALSO PREPARING FOR THE NEXT SURGE, WHICH COULD TAKE PLACE IN ANOTHER 30 YEARS. ■

Satellites: New Tools *for* New Explorations

HOW DO YOU THINK THIS PHOTOGRAPH WAS TAKEN? YOU CAN TELL THAT IT WAS TAKEN FROM ABOVE, LOOKING DOWN ON THE CITY. IN FACT, IT WAS TAKEN FROM HIGH ABOVE EARTH. SATELLITES ORBITING EARTH, WITH CAMERAS ONBOARD, TAKE PICTURES FROM SPACE. THESE CAMERAS CAN SEE MORE THAN WE CAN WITH OUR EYES ALONE.

The satellite image above shows buildings in Tampa, Florida. You can see them very clearly. Some people are interested in looking at images like this because they show where the most buildings are and where there is still room for new buildings. ▶

Sensors on the satellite can pick up different kinds of plants, along with volcanoes.

Satellite images reveal different kinds of information. The satellite image above is of the island of Hawaii. Devices called sensors, found on some satellites, can detect the difference between types of plants. They also can show where volcanoes are located. The green areas in the image above indicate where plants grow; the brown areas are volcanoes.

Uncovering New Information

Sometimes satellites discover things that people didn't know about. That's what happened when scientists began studying a portion of the Sahara Desert in Egypt. Ted Maxwell, a geologist from the Smithsonian Institution's National Air and Space Museum, is part of a team of scientists investigating what lies beneath the sands of the Sahara. They are able to see under the sand by using radar beamed from satellites orbiting above.

The images taken with radar reveal a different desert from the one we see today. They show places where streams once flowed. No one can see these areas from the ground. The satellite images on the next page show what the Sahara looks like today and what it looked like in the past.

These images made Maxwell and his fellow geologists look at the Sahara in a new light. They realized that the land had been shaped by rivers. Near these old river areas, scientists made another interesting find—objects left by people.

Scientists found stone tools and seeds of crops. It appeared as though people once lived here. During that time, the Sahara wasn't a desert. People could farm and grow enough food to live. They probably stayed until the land became hot and dry. Then they moved to the valley of the Nile River, where there was plenty of water. This new information is helping anthropologists and archaeologists—scientists who study past cultures—better understand how climate has affected people throughout history.

More Questions

Since geologists first made these discoveries, they have been mapping the areas where rivers once flowed. They are trying to figure out when the Sahara was wet and when it became so dry. ▶

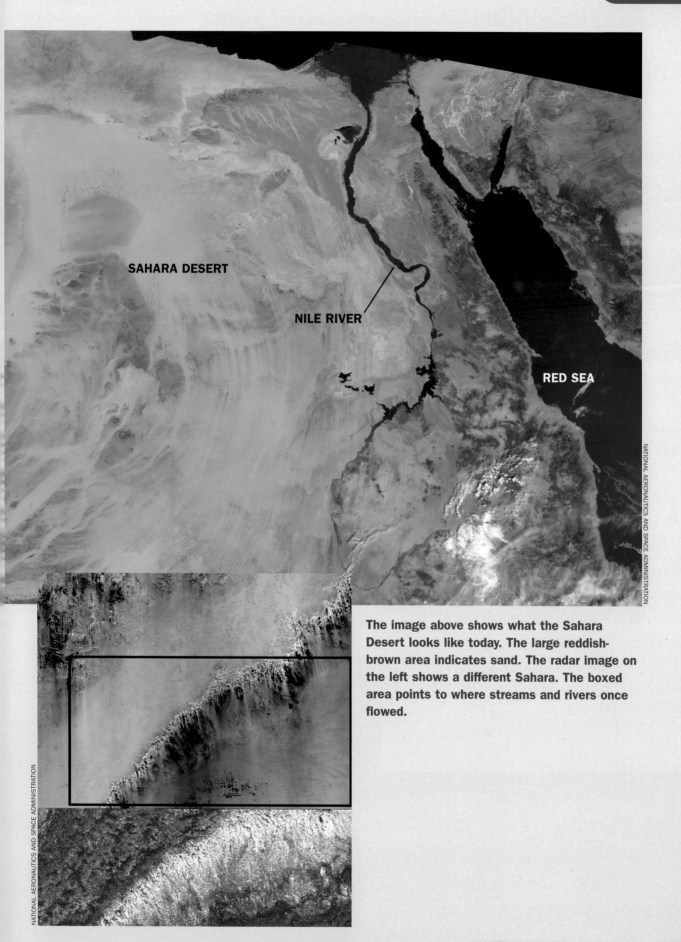

SAHARA DESERT

NILE RIVER

RED SEA

The image above shows what the Sahara Desert looks like today. The large reddish-brown area indicates sand. The radar image on the left shows a different Sahara. The boxed area points to where streams and rivers once flowed.

This is one of the largest riverbeds that can be seen on the surface of the Sahara. Others have been buried by the sand. Scientists look for signs of past human activity in areas like this one.

By digging near the old riverbeds, scientists have found old roots and grass buried in the sand. They can calculate how old the roots are. Then they have the information they need to estimate when the desert's last wet period was. They think it was more than 4,000 years ago. Before that, the desert had a dry period that lasted about 100,000 years—much longer than the current dry period has lasted.

Geologists have many questions about the Sahara. They want to know which way the old rivers flowed. They are curious about where all the sand and rocks came from. They wonder whether they were brought in with moving water, or whether the wind blew in the sand and rock from far away.

Geologists still don't know the answers to their questions, but new tools such as satellites are helping them learn more. By using new technology, geologists are uncovering the secrets of the Sahara. ■

Here's a photo of Earth from space. Pictures like this one are used to show storms and weather patterns.

PORTRAIT GALLERY, SMITHSONIAN INSTITUTION, 79-245

Joseph Henry:
The Father of Weather Forecasting

Two hundred years ago, people really didn't know how to forecast the weather. Meteorology, the study of the weather, was a new but growing field of science. Even farmers and ship captains, people who depended on the weather for their jobs, were on their own. They observed the clouds and watched how the wind was blowing. Sometimes they could tell what the weather would be like. But often they were wrong.

Then a scientist named Joseph Henry came along. He established ways to predict the weather. That's why he's called the "father of weather forecasting."

Early Weather Observations

Henry believed that scientists had learned a lot about the weather. He thought that this knowledge could help improve weather forecasting. His goal was to develop a system of weather observations. Observing the weather nationally, he thought, could solve "the problem of American storms."

Like any good scientist, Henry developed a plan of action. First, he needed weather information from around the country. So he contacted about 150 volunteer observers. Over time, the number grew to about 600. The Smithsonian supplied the volunteers with instructions, forms to use for their observations, and, in some cases, instruments. The volunteers handed in monthly weather reports from their area. The reports included information on temperature, wind and cloud conditions, and the amount of rain and snow that fell each year. The volunteers also included information on humidity, or the amount of water vapor in the air. ▶

Above: Joseph Henry had many different jobs. In addition to being a scientist, he was the first director of the Smithsonian Institution—the national museum of the United States located in Washington, D.C.

The telegraph was the new technology of the day. With a tap of a telegraph key, operators could send weather information almost anywhere.

Scientists spent years studying this information. They learned a lot from it. The information helped them better understand storms and climate differences across the country.

Telegraph a Forecast?

Henry's plan also involved weather forecasting. He used the new technology of the time—the telegraph. He arranged for nearly 20 telegraph stations around the country to report weather information to the Smithsonian once a day.

Henry posted this information on a large map at the Smithsonian Institution. He put white markers on cities with clear skies and blue markers on those with snow. Black markers pointed to places with rain, and brown markers showed those with cloudy skies. Under Henry's direction, the Smithsonian Institution had set up a way to show the weather across the country.

People were fascinated with this map. They became excited about the weather. Then government officials began discussing how to set up a national weather service. This service could keep track of the weather for everyone in the United States. Henry also hired a scientist to put the weather information into useful reports. These reports were published in 1861.

Joseph Henry's weather map posted at the Smithsonian Institution

New Information Leads to New Ideas

With so much information now available, scientists came up with new ideas about the weather. Henry thought that local storms were part of larger weather systems. Another scientist showed that storms move across the country from west to east. With this understanding, a storm's path could be plotted on a map. This finding was important. It showed Henry and other scientists that communities could be warned about storms moving their way. The telegraph could be used to warn people of storms.

In 1857, Henry was going to set up a storm warning system. But then the Civil War broke out. Henry's plan was put on hold. Soldiers needed the telegraph for the war. But after the war was over, Henry suggested that the government set up a national weather service. That's exactly what happened.

Today's weather service is very different from Henry's system. Yet his vision of how to keep track of the weather laid the foundation for the advanced weather forecasting systems we use today. ■

Bob Ryan is a meteorologist.
He also gives weather forecasts on television.

What's the Forecast?

What will the weather be like today? We all want to know, so we turn on the radio or television. We listen to a weather forecaster, or a meteorologist, like Bob Ryan. Bob works in Washington, D.C. You probably have someone just like him where you live.

Meteorologists like Bob are scientists who study the weather. They are interested in figuring out what the weather will be like the next day, the day after that, and even two or three days after that. How does Bob do it?

Gathering Information

First, Bob studies weather information from more than 3,500 weather stations. Every hour, these stations provide key information about the weather. What does Bob look for? He's interested in temperature, the direction the wind is blowing, and where rain or snow is falling. Bob and other meteorologists also collect information on humidity. Humidity is the amount of water vapor in the air. Water vapor is water in the form of a gas.

Finally, Bob pays close attention to air pressure. Although we can't see air, it has weight that presses down on everything on Earth. Air pressure has a lot do with the weather. When the air pressure is high, the weather is usually sunny. When it is low, that means that rain or snow may fall.

All these measurements are sent to the National Weather Service in Silver Spring, Maryland. There, computers put the measurements on weather maps. The maps show what weather is like around the world. ▶

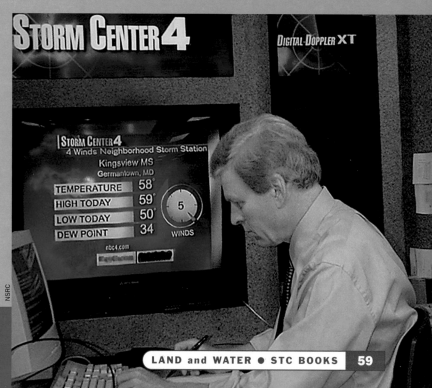

NSRC

Most television stations have weather centers like this one. Here, Bob studies weather information to figure out whether a storm is coming.

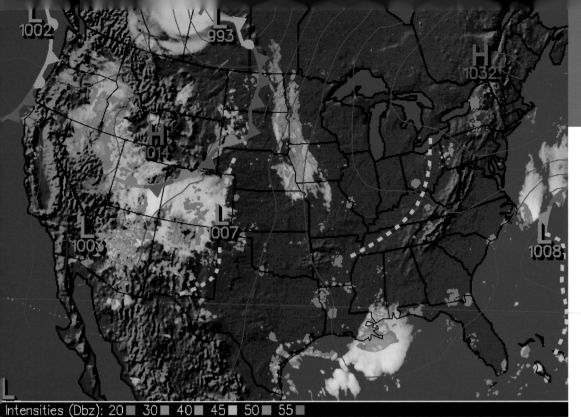

Intensities (Dbz): 20 ■ 30 ■ 40 ■ 45 ■ 50 ■ 55 ■

Meteorologists also use even more advanced tools that provide information about storms that may be coming in. Weather balloons carry instruments up into the sky to get information about the weather. Satellites take images of what Earth looks like from high in the sky. These pictures show clouds covering the planet. Looking at these images can reveal how storms, such as hurricanes, may travel.

Bob studies these maps very carefully. He needs to know what is happening far away to predict weather in the Washington, D.C., area. When Bob is ready with his forecast, he works with another meteorologist. Together, they create the weather map that is shown on television. That's how you learn what the weather is going to be like.

Weather Instruments

Do you know how meteorologists collect information about the weather? They use special weather instruments. You've probably heard of some of these instruments. What instrument tells us how hot or cold it is outside? A thermometer, of course. An instrument called an anemometer gives information about the speed of the wind. A barometer measures air pressure.

▼ **THIS SATELLITE PICTURE SHOWS HURRICANE FLOYD APPROACHING THE COAST OF FLORIDA.** The center of the hurricane is called the eye. The calm eye is surrounded by the eyewall, where the winds are the strongest.

Radar is another tool that meteorologists

NATIONAL OCEANIC AND ATMOSPHERIC ADMINIS

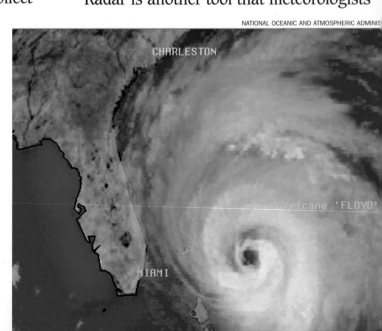

Alaska

NATIONAL OCEANIC AND ATMOSPHERIC ADMINISTRATION

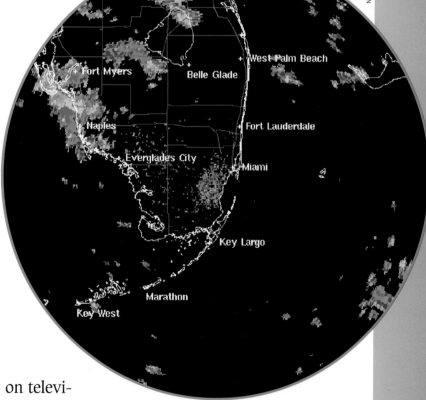

use. While satellites take pictures of weather conditions, radar uses radio waves. When the radar picks up activity, such as a storm, the instrument sends a signal as a series of beeps.

This map shows all the different parts of the country that use radar.

▲ EACH DOT STANDS FOR A WEATHER RADAR STATION.

▶ TAKE THE DOT IN MIAMI, FLORIDA. HERE'S WHAT KIND OF PICTURES THE RADAR CAN TAKE THERE.

THE COLORED AREAS SHOW PLACES WHERE IT IS RAINING.

The next time you see a weather map on television, think about what meteorologists had to do to create it. What information did they use? What instruments collected it? Why do meteorologists need so much information to predict the weather? ■

Exploring Land and Water

THAT'S A FACT!   John Wesley Powell was a determined man who made up his mind to explore the Grand Canyon.

I KNOW THAT ONE!   What is the word used to describe caving? What do cavers look for?

WHAT DO YOU THINK?   How has weather forecasting changed over the past 130 years? Has the quality of weather forecasts changed as well? Support your answer with evidence from the story.